Monmouth Park

THE SHORE'S GREATEST STRETCH SINCE 1870

Text by Sophia Mangalee
Introduction by Jerry Izenberg

This wonderful photo history of beautiful Monmouth Park, the Resort of Racing, is dedicated to the millions of passionate Thoroughbred racing fans whose unwavering support has made this history possible. Thank you all!

Special thanks to Sophia Mangalee for her hard work and dedication on this project. Additional thanks go out to the wonderful photographers who captured the great moments in Monmouth Park history: Equi-Photo (Bill Denver), Turfotos (Jim Raftery) and © Breeders' Cup Limited All Rights Reserved.

This book was made possible by Monmouth Park and *The Star-Ledger*. A portion of the proceeds from each book sold will be donated to ReRun.

Published by Pediment Publishing, a division of The Pediment Group, Inc. www.pediment.com Printed in Canada

TABLE OF CONTENTS

ReRun

ReRun's mission is to help former racehorses find a second career with caring, qualified adopters.

History and Philosophy

ReRun, Inc., was founded in 1996 in Kentucky as a non-profit 501c3 Thoroughbred adoption program and currently operates chapters in Kentucky, New Jersey and New York. Our mission is to help former racehorses find a second career by placing them in good adoptive homes.

Rather than simply retiring racehorses permanently, ReRun has promoted the versatility of Thoroughbreds in all types of riding, and matches the physical conditions and temperaments of former runners with the experience and desires of prospective adopters. Many horses coming off the racetrack have physical problems that may require rest, veterinary assistance or rehabilitation. ReRun provides former racehorses with rehabilitation by using volunteers, specialists and professionals experienced in horsemanship so these Thoroughbreds can have useful second careers. ReRun has placed hundreds of former racehorses in caring, adoptive homes as hunters, jumpers, dressage, and eventing as well as pleasure and other aspects of riding. ReRun works closely with other rescue and retirement organizations to place horses whose physical condition make a future under tack unlikely.

Thank You

We appreciate the opportunity to partner with Monmouth Park and the Star-Ledger on this wonderful book to raise money and awareness for our organization. We continually work towards the education of retired Thoroughbreds, and Monmouth Park has always been a valued partner in this endeavor.

On the opposite page you'll find a Moneigh™ from Holy Bull. These prints are original works of art done by the Thoroughbred champions to help raise money for ReRun, Inc. It's a unique way of remembering your favorite horses, as well as contributing to a worthy cause.

Thank you for your contribution to ReRun through the purchase of this book.

OPPOSITE: Moneigh™ by Holy Bull.

INTRODUCTION

In 1894, the New Jersey State Legislature was overcome by the numbing light of a retroactive epiphany. A mere 274 years after the Pilgrims landed at Plymouth Rock, the bluenoses who ran the state suddenly decided that the Pilgrims were right and outlawed all forms of gambling, proving once again that the gap between its citizens and their representatives is often just slightly less than the mileage between Trenton and Saturn.

With several pen strokes, they wiped out the original Monmouth Park, one of the finest racing plants of the time, and conversely earned the ferocious joy and gratitude of New Jersey's illegal bookmakers.

And so it remained until 1946.

Enter, Amory Haskell, the man for whom one of North America's two richest invitational horse races is

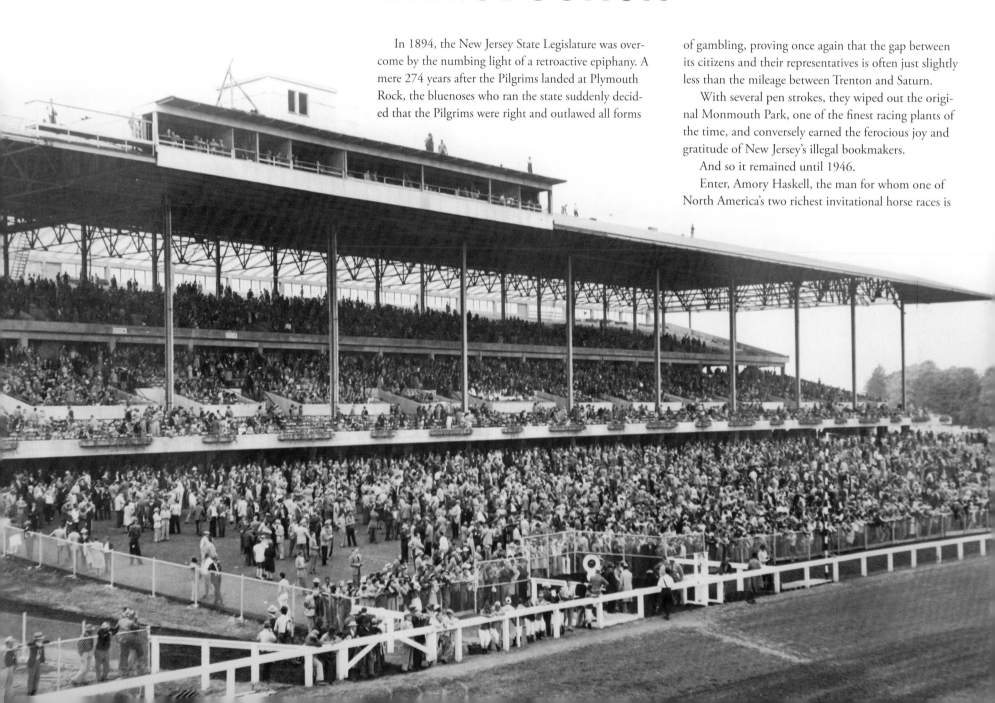

named … a man who knew which doorbells to ring, which arms to twist and how to run a racetrack as it should be run. He got the Constitution of the State of New Jersey changed. He knew which legislators' arms to twist to get the license that sealed the deal. He knew what to do when money got tight — visit a man named Philip H. Iselin.

Iselin, who made millions in the garment center, had a home adjacent to the racetrack construction.

"I hope we are not inconveniencing you too much," Amory said, concern written all over both his face and tone of voice. "Not at all," Iselin replied. "As a matter of fact, I was wishing I could join you."

"I thought," Haskell said but not too quickly, "you'd never ask." Iselin was an investor before opening day.

The track opened as a picture-postcard of a racetrack a couple of miles from the ocean … a mosaic of lazy summer afternoons punctuated by a tote board and the kind of equine history that Churchill Downs wouldn't acknowledge even with an asterisk alongside the name. But despite all that, it remained an attraction looking for its moment … the moment that would move its stature from the nearby Garden State Parkway all the way across the National map of racing.

When it came, the Ghost of Amory Haskell triggered it.

The track had named a race after him, and for 19 years it had been an event that was all dressed up for headlines with no horses to take it there. In 1987, Amory's race at Amory's track exploded into national headlines. In a single, spectacular race they brought to New Jersey the moment that launched a spectacular tradition where once had been just another feature race. They gave us a stretch run that year that clearly stands alone as New Jersey's finest racing moment.

Three horses for the ages: Bet Twice, winner of the Belmont Stakes; Alysheba, winner of the Kentucky Derby and the Preakness; Lost Code, a speedball out of Chicago, who came as an advertised rabbit but raced like a lion. Three horses that set a standard by which all Haskells must be measured and by which all others never quite seem to generate that special kind of thunder and lightning.

They came for a horse race. They gave us a three-horse photo finish and it was even closer than that.

The record book says that 20th running of the Haskell was won by the gritty Bet Twice with Alysheba a neck back and Lost Code a neck back of Alysheba. That's like saying the track was fast, the race was great and a good time was had by all.

If that's all the record book has to say, then you can mark it down in bold, capital letters that the record book is a liar, a fraud and as myopic as an over-aged bat. What happened as they thundered down the stretch that day was a hell of a lot more.

What it was, was Zale and Graziano toe-to-toe and refusing to blink. It was Jim Brown with the ball on the Giants' 5-yard line and Sam Huff, Andy Robustelli and Rosey Grier coming up to meet him with blood in their eyes. It was strength against strength, sinew against sinew and heart against heart.

It was a dead-on look into the soul of a world Black Beauty never saw and Pegasus never made. It was 12 of the gamest legs this side of the Centipede That Ate Rio.

There was Lost Code, the speedball who, by New Jersey racing law, was off Lasix for the first time and, therefore, supposed to die as they headed for home — maybe. There was Alysheba, who came up short when he could have won the Triple Crown so he could not possibly be as good as advertised — maybe. And there was Bet Twice, whose chief second, Bob Levy had said "our horse was 8-1 in the Belmont (which he won) and he didn't seem to know the difference" — and nobody could argue that point.

What they showed 32,836 that day was good enough to make another 50,000 claim in later years that they had been there, too. And even before they went to the post, the tote board clearly reflected that everyone in the joint expected this to be a horse race.

The way they bet was testimony enough. Bet Twice went off at 13-10, Alysheba at 3-2 and Lost Code at 2-1. The numbers were enough to make every pilgrim in the joint feel that maybe — just maybe — the closeness of that split promised something very special.

From the start, Lost Code went after it, and he held that lead going into the final turn. Meanwhile, Craig Perret aboard Bet Twice, and Chris McCarron, up on Alysheba, were determined to keep Lost Code honest. Both jocks knew that to ignore him was to let him steal the race.

They made him run and he ran like hell, pulling them along with him.

So this is how they rushed to history, dragging this racetrack behind them into a spotlight that is now an annual happening. Lost Code was game but about to be beaten. As for the other two, McCarron made a brilliant move to the outside despite the sharp angle and began to cut the gap between him and Bet Twice.

Down the stretch they came, with Alysheba gaining ground. Then Perret hit Bet Twice four times with the whip. On the fifth swing, he raised the little bat to the sky in triumph, trumpeting what the photo would later confirm.

Bet Twice had won.

But there's a lot more history here than that.

Turn the page and find out for yourself.

— Jerry Izenberg

THE BEGINNING

Monmouth Park's long and storied history dates back to July 30, 1870 when the track opened, just three miles from Long Branch. The track was a result of the innovative ideas of New York businessman John F. Chamberlain, New Jersey Senate President Amos Robbins and Adams Express Company President John Hoey to increase summer trade for the once bustling shore communities.

Their vision became a reality, and Monmouth Park opened its inaugural five-day meet amid much national fanfare. Due to the high caliber of its racing, Monmouth Park achieved distinction as the "Newmarket of America"– a reference to the famed racecourse in England.

Three years after the first Monmouth Park opened, financial difficulties forced the track to close. Racing returned to Monmouth Park under a syndicate of George L. Lorillard, D.D. Withers, G.P. Wetmore and James Gordon Bennett. They spent four years restoring the grounds and rebuilding the grandstand and in

1882, Monmouth Park reopened its gates. Due to its overwhelming popularity, a new racecourse was built adjacent to the existing track, and in 1890 the second Monmouth Park racetrack opened.

Monmouth Park's gates were not open for long. In 1891, the Monmouth Park meet was moved to Jerome Park and Morris Park in New York while state legislation tried to suppress pari-mutuel wagering. The state was ultimately successful, and on March 21, 1894, banned wagering on horses. The track was closed and the land sold. Racing would not return for more than 50 years. ■

LEFT: Artist rendering of the Continental Stakes heat at the grand opening of Monmouth Park, July 30, 1870. The Continental Stakes was run in mile heats with a winner's purse of $800.

RIGHT: *Spirit of the Times – A Chronicle of the Turf, Field Sports, Literature and the Stage* front page, July 8, 1882, announcing the opening of the rebuilt Monmouth Park.

ABOVE: The first Monmouth Park. John F. Chamberlain was inspired to build the track after a foxhunt in the area in 1865. The original park sat on 128 acres.

OPPOSITE: Hurdlers clear the final fence in a race at the first Monmouth Park. At that time the American Flag that flew from its roof had just 37 stars. The original mile oval was 80 feet wide and the 7,000-seat grandstand was 700 feet in length, offering a view of the entire course. Women were allowed to wager and could hire escorts to purchase tickets, assist in finding their seats and provide physical protection.

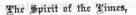

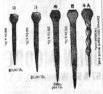

LEFT: Advertisements from the June 17, 1882 *Spirit of the Times* reflect an era ruled by the horse. Horseshoe nails, family carriages and wagons were among a few of the advertisements that took priority.

ABOVE: The grandstand after being devastated by a storm in 1899.
Courtesy U.S. Army CECOM LCMC History Office

RIGHT: A view of the Monmouth Park Hotel looking east, circa 1890.
Courtesy U.S. Army CECOM LCMC History Office

ABOVE: President Ulysses S. Grant, a boxholder, was a frequent visitor to Monmouth Park and Long Branch. The track owners, in an effort to generate larger crowds, placed a statue of President Grant in front of the grandstand hoping passersbys would come in to potentially catch a glimpse of the President.

TOP RIGHT: Monmouth Park was located two-and-a-half hours from New York City and three hours from Philadelphia by carriage. In season, two steamboats made daily runs from Pier 28 in New York to Sandy Hook. From there, patrons could make the rest of the trip on rail. The round trip was said to cost less than two dollars.

RIGHT: Drawing of the original Monmouth Park gates. The wooden arches were located on today's Broad Street, near Park Avenue, in Long Branch.

LEFT: Salvator (inside) was a national hero. He won the Suburban Handicap by a neck over Tenney, and a match race was proposed to decide the better horse. In the match race, Salvator's fractional times equaled the American records for seven, eight and nine furlongs. At the wire, Salvator beat Tenney by a nose in an American record of 2:05 for a mile and a quarter, and he would best Tenney again in the Champion Stakes. The two raced against time in special separate events to try to beat the American record of 1:39 ¼ for the mile. Tenney was clocked at 1:40 3/4, but three days later, Salvator blazed the mile in 1:35 1/2 over the straight Monmouth course. The Salvator Mile is run each season at Monmouth Park to honor this great runner's achievement.

BOTTOM LEFT: This coach left daily from the Hollowood Hotel for the races at Monmouth Park. When not chartered, single seats could be obtained. Pictured are Lewis Thomson of Brookdale; "Abe" Hummel of How and Hummel; John Hoey, President of Adams Express; Andrew Freedman of early baseball fame and B. Altman & Co; Fred Hoey, international pigeon shot; Joseph Morro of Havana and John S. Hoey, actor.

BELOW: The second Monmouth Park opened July 4, 1890. The enormous structure, touted as the largest racetrack in the world, was made entirely of iron and measured 1,100 feet from the end of the grandstand to the tip of the clubhouse. Built on the cantilever truss system, it was the only one of its kind in the country. The track closed in 1894 due to anti-gambling legislation, and five years later, the once magnificent grandstand was decimated by a storm.

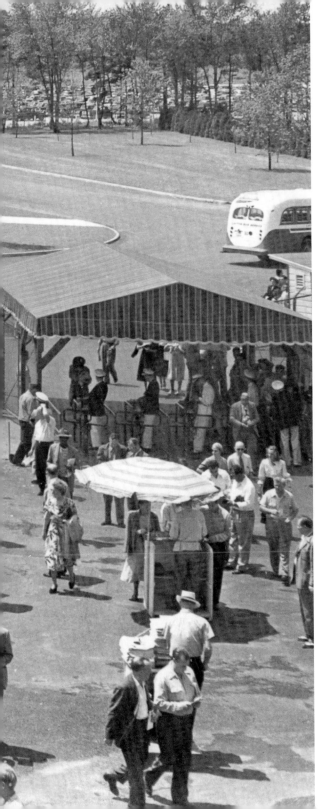

THE MONMOUTH PARK JOCKEY CLUB ERA 1946 AND ON

During the 1940's, Amory L. Haskell played a major part in lobbying to legalize pari-mutuel wagering for both the standardbred and Thoroughbred industries. On June 19, 1946, for the third time and following a 53-year hiatus, Monmouth Park reopened its doors. Under the new leadership of Haskell, Philip H. Iselin, Reeve Schley, Joseph M. Roebling, Townsend B. Martin, John MacDonald and James Cox Brady, the Monmouth Park Jockey Club was born.

Iselin became chairman of the construction committee and was named treasurer of the Monmouth Park Jockey Club. After Amory Haskell's death, Phillip H. Iselin assumed the track presidency.

Opening day attracted 18,724 attendees, and Monmouth Park returned to a level of glory and prestige that had only been a memory. The first horse on the grounds was Ship Ahoy, who arrived from Mexico for owner Mrs. L. V. Bellew of Chicago. Jockey Nick Jemas won two races that day including the opener aboard Blind Path. Modern day stakes races, including the Molly Pitcher Handicap and the Lamplighter, held their inaugural runnings in 1946, with the Monmouth Oaks and Colleen Stakes continuing their popularity from the 1800's.

The New Jersey Sports and Exposition Authority purchased Monmouth Park in 1986 and many of the historic, century-old stakes races were reinstated, with the Monmouth Cup, inaugurated in 1884, renamed the Philip H. Iselin Handicap. ∎

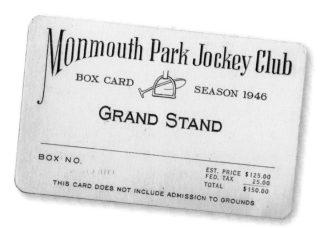

LEFT: Monmouth Park, 1948.

RIGHT: Monmouth Park Jockey Club Box Card for the inaugural 1946 season.

LEFT: Aerial view of construction of Monmouth Park.

BOTTOM LEFT: Construction of the administration building and the adjacent saddling paddock. A library was later added to the two-story administration building.

ABOVE: Tractors and rollers lay down the dirt oval at the third Monmouth Park.

BELOW: Sketch of the new grandstand entrance. The same turnstiles from 1946 are still in use today.

OPPOSITE: The field thunders down the homestretch before a packed house.

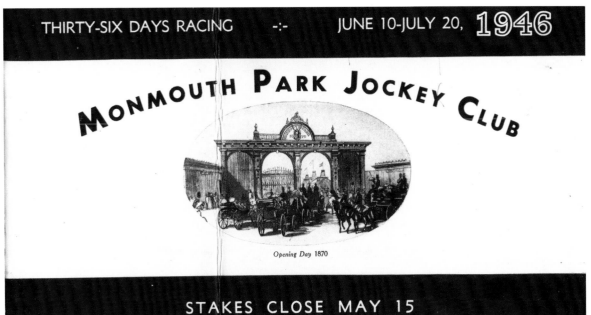

THIRTY-SIX DAYS RACING   -:-   JUNE 10-JULY 20, 1946

MONMOUTH PARK JOCKEY CLUB

Opening Day 1870

STAKES CLOSE MAY 15

OPPOSITE TOP LEFT: Field rounds the clubhouse turn.

OPPOSITE BOTTOM LEFT: Crowd exits the Pony Express at Monmouth Park. The rail line ran directly into the track and provided service from New York City until the late 1990's.

OPPOSITE RIGHT: The train carries hundreds of patrons to Monmouth Park.

TOP LEFT: A sea of cars parked at Monmouth Park, 1950's.

BOTTOM LEFT: Cover of the 1946 Stakes Book. The Monmouth Park Jockey Club continued the symbolic tradition of the original arched gates from 1870 although they were not constructed at the third Monmouth Park.

BELOW: A $2 exacta ticket from the 1970's.

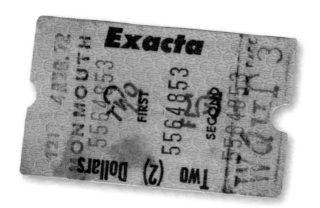

STAKES TO BE RUN DURING SUMMER MEETING 1949

ENTRIES CLOSE Wednesday, June 1, 1949

Saturday, June 18 ____THE SALVATOR MILE, Three-Year-Olds and Upward—One Mile ____$10,000 ADDED

Saturday, June 25 ____THE SELECT HANDICAP, Three-Year-Olds—Six Furlongs ____$10,000 ADDED

Wednesday, June 29____THE REGRET HANDICAP, Fillies and Mares—Three-Year-Olds and Upward—Six Furlongs ____$10,000 ADDED

Saturday, July 2 ____THE LONG BRANCH HANDICAP, Three-Year-Olds and Upward—One Mile and a Sixteenth ____$10,000 ADDED

Monday, July 4 ____THE COLLEEN STAKES, Fillies, Two-Years-Old—Five and a Half Furlongs ____$10,000 ADDED

Saturday, July 9 ____THE RUMSON HANDICAP, Three-Year-Olds and Upward—Six Furlongs ____$10,000 ADDED

Wednesday, July 13 ____THE NEW JERSEY FUTURITY, Two-Year-Olds, Five and a Half Furlongs (Jersey Foaled) ____$10,000 ADDED

Saturday, July 16 ____THE LAMPLIGHTER HANDICAP, Three-Year-Olds—One Mile and a Sixteenth ____$15,000 ADDED

Wednesday, July 20 ____THE MONMOUTH OAKS, Fillies, Three-Year-Olds—One Mile and a Sixteenth ____$10,000 ADDED

Saturday, July 23 ____THE MONMOUTH HANDICAP, Three-Year-Olds and Upward—One Mile and a Quarter ____$25,000 ADDED

Wednesday, July 27 ____THE SAPLING STAKES, Two-Year-Olds—Six Furlongs ____$10,000 ADDED

Saturday, July 30 ____THE MOLLY PITCHER HANDICAP, Fillies and Mares, Three-Year-Olds and Upward
One Mile and a Sixteenth ____$15,000 ADDED

Wednesday, Aug. 3____THE OCEANPORT HANDICAP, Three-Year-Olds and Upward—Six Furlongs ____$10,000 ADDED

Saturday, Aug. 6 ____THE CHOICE STAKES, Three-Year-Olds—One Mile and a Quarter ____$25,000 ADDED

Wednesday, Aug. 10 ____THE OMNIBUS HANDICAP, Three-Year-Olds and Upward—One Mile and a Furlong ____$15,000 ADDED

OPPOSITE: Aerial view of Monmouth Park from the 1950's shows a packed grandstand and parking lot.

TOP LEFT: Horses round the clubhouse turn in the shadow of the Parterres. The Parterre boxes were the first luxury suites ever built in North America. The third level was added in 1951.

BOTTOM LEFT: The 1949 Monmouth Park Jockey Club stakes schedule. The Salvator Mile opened the season. Every stakes race run in 1949 continues to be run today. The Choice Stakes would later be renamed The Haskell, and the Choice Stakes would continue as a turf race for three-year-olds.

ABOVE: Inside rail shot. The original railing was constructed of wood. A safety rail was installed in the late 1980's.

BELOW: First race of the 1954 racing season.

OPPOSITE LEFT: Amory Haskell with the 1955 Monmouth Handicap Trophy.

OPPOSITE RIGHT: Amory Haskell (center) presents the 1950 Monmouth Park leading jockey award to Jimmy Stout (left) and the leading trainer award to Daverne "Dave" Emery (right). Jimmy Stout, a New Jersey native, won four riding titles at Monmouth Park. He was a 1968 inductee into the National Museum of Racing and Hall of Fame. Emery also won four titles, the last to come in 1957 despite dying of a heart attack August 6 of that year.

TOP LEFT: Philip H. Iselin in the library at Monmouth Park. The library, still in use today, houses collections of the *Turf Registry* and *Racing Manual* dating back to the early 1800's.

BOTTOM LEFT: Philip H. Iselin at Monmouth Park. Iselin held the position of president and chairman of the board from 1966 until his death in 1976. Under Iselin, Monmouth Park established many firsts: videotape patrol, a nationally televised race, an interior chute for the grass course, a turf club in the grandstand, a recreation hall in the stable area and a modern air-conditioned press box.

ABOVE: Marion Twaddell (left), secretary of Helis Stock Farm, and Philip H. Iselin (right), president of Monmouth Park Jockey Club, make a presentation at the annual yearling show. The filly, Bold Fluff by Boldnesian-Cherry Fluff by Sohoes, would go on to produce Bold Rendevous, third in the Grade I Kentucky Oaks.

ABOVE: Pool area at Monmouth Park. The Olympic-sized pool was installed under the direction of Philip H. Iselin and was located adjacent to the jockey's room.

TOP RIGHT: Pierre Bellocq created many caricatures of the American Turf, and Monmouth Park was no exception. This drawing was done for the 1977 Haskell, formerly the Monmouth Invitational, won by Silver Series.

BOTTOM RIGHT: Horse-drawn carriage delivers its passengers to the Monmouth Park winner's circle.

BELOW: Bathing beauty with her horse at the pool.

OPPOSITE: Swimmers prepare to dive into the pool at Monmouth Park. The pool was removed in 2007 in preparation for the Breeders' Cup World Championships.

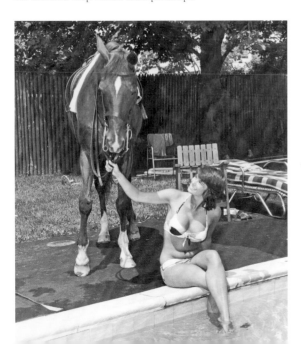

OPPOSITE: Horses break from the gate in the 5-½ furlong turf chute. The chute was installed in 2006 along with a new turf course in preparation for the 2007 Breeders' Cup World Championships. Turf racing began at Monmouth Park in 1950 and the 1/8th-mile turf chute was added in 1967 to give patrons a head-on view of the horses approaching the stands.

LEFT: Thoroughbreds enter the clubhouse turn at Monmouth Park.

ABOVE: Thoroughbred action at Monmouth Park.

FOLLOWING LEFT: A groom leads his charge from the paddock, through the tunnel, to the main track. Pedro Cotto, Jr. is in the irons.

FOLLOWING RIGHT: Horses circle the English-style walking ring before a race.

THE TRACK

Beautiful Monmouth Park has maintained its position among the upper echelon of the nation's premier racetracks since its inaugural race meet in 1870. Known throughout the country as the "Resort of Racing," Monmouth Park is truly a gem on the Jersey Shore. Just two miles from the sandy beaches of Long Branch, Monmouth Park continues to draw Shore tourists and locals alike to its park-like setting.

The lavish, one-of-a-kind Parterre boxes are frequented by season box-holders, while the casual fan enjoys relaxing in the expansive picnic area along the homestretch. Built in 1946, the massive grandstand takes racing fans back to a bygone era when racing was the number-one spectator sport in the world.

Now outfitted with modern-day amenities, the clubhouse sports heating in the winter and air-conditioning in the summer. Unique in its construction is the 104,000 square-foot aluminum roof (installed in 1971) covering the entire grandstand and clubhouse. Over 1,500 televisions bring races from across the nation and around the world straight to the Monmouth Park patron.

Monmouth Park has aged gracefully over the past 60 years. The green and white colors shine brightly each spring with a fresh coat of paint. Lawn jockeys welcome racing patrons with the colors of the grand racing stables, while the freshly waxed floors reflect the silks of the great racehorses in the Hall of Champions.

Each year Monmouth Park awakens with new life and the heartbeat of racing hooves, providing everyone with the excitement and anticipation of a new season. ■

LEFT: A Thoroughbred powers down the mile-and-an-eighth turf chute beneath blue, summer skies.

RIGHT: Charlie and Marianne Hesse. In 1946, Charlie Hesse's construction company installed the first dirt surface at Monmouth Park.

OPPOSITE TOP LEFT: Hurdlers brush over a jump on the Monmouth Park turf course in the 1970's.

OPPOSITE BOTTOM LEFT: Horses circle the English-style walking ring in the late 1940's.

OPPOSITE RIGHT: Graceful spiral hedges sweep the turns in this aerial shot of Monmouth Park. The Shrewsbury River can be seen in the background.

LEFT: The crowd watches horses battle down Monmouth Park's stretch.

ABOVE: Foolish Pleasure captures the 1974 Sapling Stakes with Javinto Vasquez aboard. The tote board (background) was installed in 1946 and remains operational to this day. The original board only displayed payouts for win, place and show. As exotic wagers were added, the payouts were incorporated on the matrix portion of the board.

Monmouth Park

OPPOSITE TOP: Racing fans enjoy a relaxing afternoon in the picnic area. Nearly 400 umbrella-shaded picnic tables line the top of the stretch.

OPPOSITE BOTTOM: Two young racing fans inspect the Shoe Board adjacent to the saddling paddock.

FAR LEFT: Patrons watch the races from the luxury Parterre boxes. The first of their kind at a sporting venue, the private boxes seat six to eight and include full food and beverage service.

LEFT: Children enjoy the picnic area playground.

BELOW: Striped umbrellas shade race goers at the Lady's Secret Café. The café's namesake was the famous race mare Lady's Secret, who earned 1986 Horse of the Year honors. She amassed an amazing eight Grade I victories that season including Monmouth Park's Molly Pitcher Handicap in stakes record time.

ABOVE: Horses make their way through the tunnel to the paddock for saddling. The walk is known as Alibi Lane for the stories told by jockeys on their return from the track.

TOP RIGHT: The saddling enclosure. Horses are saddled under the enclosure and then paraded around the English-style walking ring before continuing to the track.

BOTTOM RIGHT: Jockeys and their mounts are led through the tunnel to the track.

OPPOSITE: A groom leads his horse around the walking ring as the jockey ties his knot. The knot is tied short and safe so that the jockey and horse do not get caught in the reins.

FAR LEFT: Horses race around the clubhouse turn. The clubhouse and grandstand seat 13,000, and the entire facility easily accommodates over 50,000.

LEFT: A Thoroughbred readies for the start. The starting gate is held closed by a magnetic current that is released at the push of the starter's button.

BELOW: A full field breaks from the starting gate.

TOP: Flags fly Monmouth Park's traditional gate logo.

ABOVE: Jockeys battle for position out of the gate.

RIGHT: Fans intently watch the racing action.

OPPOSITE: A jockey guides his mount through traffic. The jockeys wear multiple pairs of goggles that are pulled down as each pair gets dirty.

OPPOSITE: A young fan celebrates his first birthday at Monmouth Park.

LEFT: Dirt flies as horses race into the first turn.

ABOVE: Mario Madrid prepares to ride at Monmouth Park.

FOLLOWING: Horses thunder down the stretch in the 2007 Philip H. Iselin Handicap. Gottcha Gold (far right) won under jockey Chuck C. Lopez.

PEOPLE

No racetrack is complete without the colorful personalities that lend their presence to the races. Monmouth Park's own collection of personalities includes movie stars, sports legends and of course the stars of the turf — the jockeys, trainers and owners.

The jockeys steal the show every raceday with their courage and competitive spirit. Though small of stature, they are big of heart when guiding half-ton animals through traffic at speeds of 40 mph. The jockey colony at Monmouth Park has always been one of outstanding class and talent. Walter Blum, Sam Boulmetis, Bill Hartack, Jorge Velasquez and Julie Krone are just a few of the Hall of Fame riders to have earned riding titles at Monmouth Park.

The trainers work tirelessly seven days a week, 365 days a year. The first at the barn and the last to leave, the trainer may have over 40 horses in his care or just one. The trainer is not only responsible for the conditioning of his horses, he is also a master of public relations, managing owners, media and staff.

And of course, the owners provide the driving force behind the scenes – the much-needed capital necessary to acquire the blue-blooded horses that will carry their colors. The ultimate nod to an owner's participation is the brightly colored silks the jockeys wear, crafted in the owner's particular design, color and taste. ■

LEFT: Walter Blum's 4,000th career win came aboard Student Lamp. He became just the sixth jockey to achieve this milestone. Blum retired with 4,382 winners and was inducted into the Hall of Fame in 1987.

RIGHT: Actor Bill Murray weighs in at Monmouth Park.

ABOVE: MacKenzie Miller (left), jockey Sam Boulmetis (center), and trainer Horace A. "Jimmy" Jones (right). Jones worked as the head trainer for the famed Calumet Farm in Kentucky and had Citation, Iron Leige and Tim Tam among his Kentucky Derby winners. Upon his retirement from training in 1964, he became Monmouth Park's Director of Racing.

RIGHT: Ogden Phipps and his mother, Mrs. Henry Carnegie Phipps, in the paddock.

OPPOSITE: James Edward "Sunny Jim" Fitzsimmons celebrates his 83rd birthday at Monmouth Park. Among his numerous accomplishments, Mr. Fitz trained two Triple Crown winners, Gallant Fox in 1930 and Omaha in 1935.

OPPOSITE: Jack Leonard, Tommy Root, Sam Boulmetis and Dick Lawlers surround actress and singer Constance Towers. Towers' noted films include *The Horse Soldiers* (1959) and *Shock Corridor* (1963).

LEFT: Peggy Lee goes over the day's races with Monmouth Park jockeys.

ABOVE: A jockey enjoys quality time with a lovely group of ladies.

TOP LEFT: Walt Michaels (left), defensive coach of the New York Jets, and head coach Wilbur "Weeb" Ewbank fit a jockey with a Jets helmet.

BOTTOM LEFT: Jockey Logan Batcheller gives fighter Bobo Olson a friendly punch. Bobo Olson was the world middleweight champion 1953-1955.

ABOVE: Jockey Kevin Daly and Mike Miceli (inside) are filmed during the making of a TV commercial for a candy bar sponsor. It showed the "wrong way" rider munching a candy bar while riding in this unorthodox fashion.

OPPOSITE: Hall of Fame jockeys Walter Blum and Sam Boulmetis cool off. Boulmetis won four riding titles at Monmouth Park in the 1940's and '50's.

OPPOSITE TOP LEFT: New Jersey Governor Alfred E. Driscoll watches a race with Amory L. Haskell. Driscoll served as governor from 1947-1954. He was the chief proponent of the New Jersey Turnpike and the Garden State Parkway.

OPPOSITE BOTTOM LEFT: TV host Barbara Luna interviews Joe Bravo in the paddock prior to a race.

OPPOSITE RIGHT: Paul Whiteman expresses concern on the scale in the jockey's room. Whiteman was dubbed the "King of Jazz" in the 1920's and "Paul Whiteman and his Orchestra" starred in *King of Jazz*, the first feature-length musical movie filmed entirely in Technicolor.

ABOVE: Little Big Chief looks over the entries for the 1972 $100,000 Sapling Stakes with assistant trainer Tim Raymond, son of trainer Bill Raymond.

RIGHT: Comedian Bob Hope puckers up to plant a kiss on the nose of Doctor Art after the grey gelding romped to victory in the 1973 Bob Hope Purse.

OPPOSITE: Jerry Bailey returns to the winner's circle aboard Proper Reality after winning the 1989 Philip H. Iselin Handicap. Bailey won the Iselin three times from seven mounts. He retired with 5,892 wins and was inducted into the Hall of Fame in 1995.

ABOVE: Jockey Chris Antley, who captured three consecutive riding titles at Monmouth Park in the 1980's. In 1984, at the age of 18, he booted home a Monmouth Park seasonal record 171 winners. His 469 winners that year were the most by any jockey in the country.

TOP RIGHT: Jockey Joe Bravo celebrates his 6th win on the Monmouth Park card. Bravo accomplished this feat four times at Monmouth Park.

BOTTOM LEFT: Carson City returns to the winner's circle with Hall of Fame jockey Julie Krone in the irons after winning the 1989 Sapling Stakes. In 1987, Krone made history at Monmouth Park when she became the first woman to win a riding title at a major racetrack. She also won the title the next two years.

BOTTOM RIGHT: Hall of Fame Trainer W.A. "Jimmy" Croll and rider Craig Perret observe the training of Croll horses.

TOP LEFT: Trainer John Forbes giving jockey Julie Krone instructions in the paddock. Forbes won five Monmouth Park training titles (1979, 1981, 1989, 1990, and 1991).

BOTTOM LEFT: Jockey Tanna Clark is carried to the pool by jockey Robert Colton after winning her first race aboard Drums For Love.

ABOVE: Jockeys sign autographs for the annual Don MacBeth Memorial Jockey Fund. MacBeth was a regular at Monmouth Park and earned riding titles in 1978, '79, and '80. MacBeth won 2,764 races before cancer ended his career. A fund was set up in his name by comedic actor and former exercise rider Tim Conway to assist injured and disabled riders.

OPPOSITE: Jockey Joe Bravo returns to the winner's circle. "Jersey Joe" has won an astonishing 13 riding titles at Monmouth Park.

RACEDAY

Raceday begins long before the first fans line up at the entrance gates and long before the first mutuel ticket is punched. It begins in the predawn hours before the rooster crows and most of the world awakes.

In the predawn light, Thoroughbreds munch contentedly on their morning breakfast of oats while their trainers ponder the day's training schedule. As the sun rises, the grooms pick straw from tails and saddle their charges, in preparation for the waiting jockeys and exercise riders who put their mounts through morning training.

The routine is repeated day in and day out, all in preparation for the ultimate goal — raceday. As the afternoon approaches, fans begin to line up at the gates, set on securing a picnic table with the perfect view or that favorite bench by the finish line. First stop is the program stand for the guide to the day's races, then it's handicapping time.

While the fans ponder the potential winners of the day's races, the jockeys prepare for the races ahead. The jockey's room buzzes with the easy banter of competitive natures.

Finally, it's post time! The excited horses are saddled and eagerly circle the walking ring before being united with their rider. With the jockeys finally aboard they head to the track, summoned by the call to post.

Anticipation and excitement build — tickets are clutched tightly, the horses load into the gate. Tension builds as jockeys crouch with a handful of mane and rein, ready for the gates to spring open…*they're off!* ◼

LEFT: Thoroughbreds spring into action at Monmouth Park.

RIGHT: A winning mutuel ticket.

PREVIOUS PAGE LEFT: Double Booked (inside) noses out Yankee Affair (outside) to win the 1989 $100,000 Longfellow Handicap.

PREVIOUS RIGHT: Patrons pack the Monmouth Park grandstand.

OPPOSITE: Horses pass the starter's stand. Before the invention of the electric starting gate, horses lined up behind a ribbon or rope and the race would begin when the ribbon was raised.

TOP LEFT: Director of Racing and Hall of Fame trainer Jimmy Jones shows a young fan a race saddle.

BOTTOM LEFT: Jockey Eddie Arcaro makes his way back from the track with his valet. Arcaro is the only rider to have won the Triple Crown twice, Whirlaway (1941) and Citation (1948). He rode many of Monmouth's Hall of Champions inductees including Kelso, Bold Ruler, Nashua and Sword Dancer. Arcaro was inducted into the Hall of Fame in 1958.

ABOVE: Expensive Decision, with Jean-Luc Samyn aboard, wins the 1989 Choice Handicap.

MONMOUTH
Park

JUNE 16 — AUGUST 8

1951

OFFICIAL PROGRAM

FIFTEEN CENTS

Monmouth
Park

A GREAT NAME IN AMERICAN RACING

OFFICIAL PROGRAM

1961

JUNE 9 — AUGUST 5

Third Day
Monday, June 12

TWENTY-FIVE CENTS

Monmouth
Park

THE RESORT OF RACING

OFFICIAL
PROGRAM

1963

MAY 31
•
AUGUST 3

TWENTY-FIVE CENTS

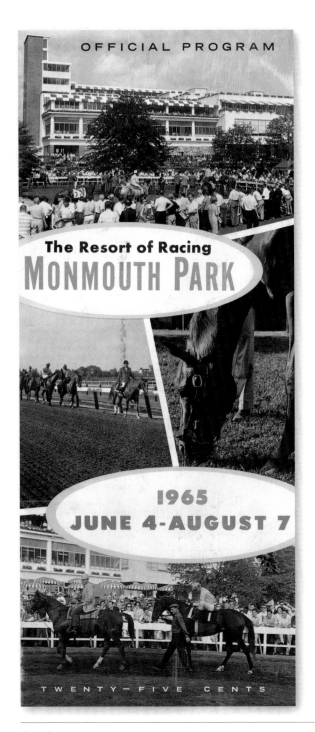

OFFICIAL PROGRAM

The Resort of Racing
MONMOUTH PARK

1965
JUNE 4-AUGUST 7

TWENTY-FIVE CENTS

Monmouth Park

A GREAT NAME IN AMERICAN RACING

1974

MAY 29 - AUGUST 10

OFFICIAL PROGRAM 35¢ TWO CENTS SALES TAX INCLUDED

Official Program

Fast Times at the Jersey Shore

THIS PAGE & OPPOSITE PAGE: Official program covers from Monmouth Park. A new cover is designed each year.

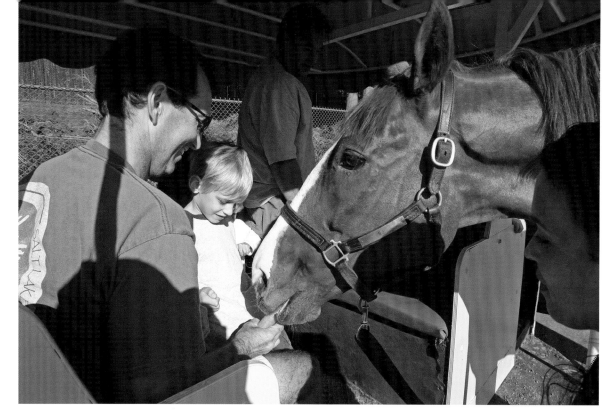

OPPOSITE: An exercise rider and his mount in the early morning light. With over 1,500 horses stabled on the grounds, hundreds of horses may be training on the track at any one time.

FAR LEFT: A Thoroughbred walks the shed row.

LEFT: A blacksmith nails on a shoe. Racing plates (shoes) are made of lightweight aluminum and are affixed by glue or nails.

ABOVE: Families feed carrots to a stable pony on the free Dawn Patrol morning tour.

OPPOSITE LEFT: A jockey's saddle lies ready. Jockey saddles weigh between one and seven pounds. Additional lead weights can be added to flaps beneath the stirrups in order to achieve the required weight.

OPPOSITE RIGHT: Silks laid out for the day's races.

TOP LEFT: Saddle towels are arranged prior to post.

BOTTOM LEFT: Arm numbers hang in a row. Jockeys wear the number on their upper arm to assist with identification during a race.

ABOVE: Jockey Eddie Castro aboard his mount in the paddock.

Monmouth Park

OPPOSITE TOP: Horsemen clean the exercise saddles after morning work. The exercise saddles are slightly larger than a jockey saddle and are three times as heavy.

OPPOSITE BOTTOM: A racehorse eyes his jockey in the paddock.

LEFT: Outriders lead the horses through the English-style walking ring and out to the track. The outrider is provided for safety and assistance in the case of an equipment failure or out-of-control horse.

ABOVE: Thoroughbreds make their way to the paddock for the next race.

Monmouth Park

PREVIOUS TOP LEFT: Jockey Luis Rivera, Jr., ready for action.

PREVIOUS BOTTOM LEFT: Saddle overgirths hang near the Jockeys' Quarters.

PREVIOUS TOP MIDDLE: Jockeys wait to make their way to the paddock.

PREVIOUS BOTTOM MIDDLE: A jockey readies his hold.

PREVIOUS RIGHT: Bugler Frank Hughes calls the horses to the post.

OPPOSITE TOP: Thoroughbreds during the post parade prior to a race.

OPPOSITE BOTTOM: The pre-race warm-up.

LEFT: A steady pony horse accompanies a racehorse during the post parade.

ABOVE: Pony horses wait for the racehorses. The pony horses escort them to the starting gate and provide a calming effect for the often-nervous racers.

FOLLOWING LEFT: Horses spring from the starting gate. Thoroughbreds can accelerate to 40 mph in just five strides.

FOLLOWING RIGHT: The homestretch of the turf course.

PREVIOUS: Haskell Day 2001.

ABOVE: A jockey urges his mount to the finish line.

RIGHT: Horses bank onto the main turf course from the 1/8th-mile chute.

OPPOSITE: Jockey Joe Bravo celebrates another win.

HALL OF CHAMPIONS

Opened in 1986 and located on the first floor of the grandstand, the Hall of Champions honors the best horses ever to compete at Monmouth Park. The banners fly the silks of the many Champions whose hooves have thundered down the Monmouth homestretch.

The hall reads like a "who's who" of racing immortals: Kelso, Ruffian, Forego, John Henry, Spectacular Bid, Alysheba, Alydar, Damascus, Lady's Secret, Buckpasser, and Personal Ensign. Twenty-five of the 58 Hall of Champions inductees also have a coveted place in the National Hall of Fame.

From the 1940's: Stymie*, Polynesian and First Flight.

From the 1950's: Blue Sparkler, Bold Ruler*, Decathlon, Helioscope, Misty Morn, Nashua*, Needles* and Sword Dancer*.

From the 1960's: Affectionately*, Buckpasser*, Carry Back*, Damascus*, Kelso*, Mongo, Politely and Ta Wee*.

From the 1970's: Alydar*, Dan Horn, Dearly Precious, Desert Vixen*, Forego*, John Henry*, Majestic Light, Riva Ridge* and Ruffian*.

From the 1980's: Alysheba*, Bet Twice, Forty Niner, Lady's Secret*, Lord Avie, Lost Code, Open Mind, Personal Ensign*, Spectacular Bid* and Spend a Buck.

From the 1990's: Black Tie Affair, Dehere, Formal Gold, Friendly Lover, Frisk Me Now, Hansel, Holy Bull*, Inside Information*, Serena's Song*, Safely Kept, Skip Away*, Smoke Glacken and Touch Gold.

From the 2000's: English Channel, Ghostzapper, Lion Heart, Point Given, Silverbulletday, War Emblem and With Anticipation. ■

*Hall of Fame member.

LEFT: The Hall of Champions stretches the length of the first floor of the grandstand.

RIGHT: Amory L. Haskell (second from right) presents the 1958 Monmouth Handicap trophy to Wheatley Stable owner Mrs. Henry Carnegie Phipps, jockey Eddie Arcaro (second from left) and trainer "Sunny Jim" Fitzsimmons (right) after Bold Ruler's victory.

TOP RIGHT: Alysheba (outside), with Chris McCarron aboard, winning the 1988 Philip H. Iselin Handicap over Bet Twice. Alysheba won the 1987 Kentucky Derby and Preakness Stakes, but lost to Bet Twice in the Belmont Stakes and Haskell Invitational. He earned Champion Three-Year-Old honors in 1987 and 1988 Horse of the Year honors.

BOTTOM RIGHT: Alysheba triumphs over fellow Hall of Champions member Bet Twice in the 1988 Philip H. Iselin Handicap. Bet Twice was owned by a syndicate of approximately three dozen individuals. The primary shareholder was Robert Levy, former owner of Atlantic City Racecourse.

BELOW: As a two-year-old, Needles won the 1955 Sapling Stakes. At three, he captured the Kentucky Derby and Belmont Stakes. He was named Needles after suffering from broken ribs and pneumonia as a foal and the subsequent vet visits. He is a member of the Hall of Champions as well as the Hall of Fame.

ABOVE: Alydar, with Eddie Maple up, returns to the winner's circle after victory in the 1977 Sapling Stakes. Alydar is a member of the Hall of Fame and Hall of Champions.

TOP RIGHT: Alydar gallops home in the slop in the 1977 Sapling Stakes. Alydar finished second behind his archrival Affirmed in each race of the 1978 Triple Crown.

BOTTOM RIGHT: Ruffian bested her rivals in the 1974 Sorority Stakes under jockey Jacinto Vasquez. Nicknamed the "Queen of Fillies," Ruffian earned Champion Two-Year-Old Filly and Champion Three-Year-Old Filly honors after starting her career with 10 straight wins.

OPPOSITE: Eleven-year-old Kelso takes a jump under Michael Plumb, Captain of the U.S. Olympic Equestrian Team, at Monmouth Park where Kelso won his first stakes victory in the 1960 Choice Stakes. The gelding showcased his multiple talents in this 1968 exhibition of dressage and jumping.

LEFT: Kelso, Bill Hartack aboard, returns to the winner's circle after defeating an allowance field by ten lengths. Kelso earned Horse of the Year honors five years in a row (1960-1964) and earned nearly $2 million in a career that stretched eight seasons. He is ranked #4 on the list of the Top 100 Thoroughbred Champions of the 20th Century by *The Blood-Horse* magazine behind only Man O' War (1st), Secretariat (2nd) and Citation (3rd).

FOLLOWING LEFT: Bold Ruler defeats Sharpsburg in the 1958 Monmouth Handicap, later renamed the Philip H. Iselin Handicap, under 134 pounds, the heaviest impost in the race's history. The Monmouth Handicap was Bold Ruler's final win before retirement. Bold Ruler enjoyed a successful career on the track, but excelled as a sire. Bold Ruler sired Triple Crown winner Secretariat and was the grandsire of such outstanding runners as Foolish Pleasure, Ruffian and Spectacular Bid.

FOLLOWING RIGHT: Bold Ruler in the Monmouth Park winner's circle with Eddie Arcaro up after winning the 1958 Monmouth Handicap. Wheatley Stable owner Mrs. H.C. Phipps is in the background. Bold Ruler earned Horse of the Year honors in 1957 as well as Champion Sprinter and Champion Three-Year-Old.

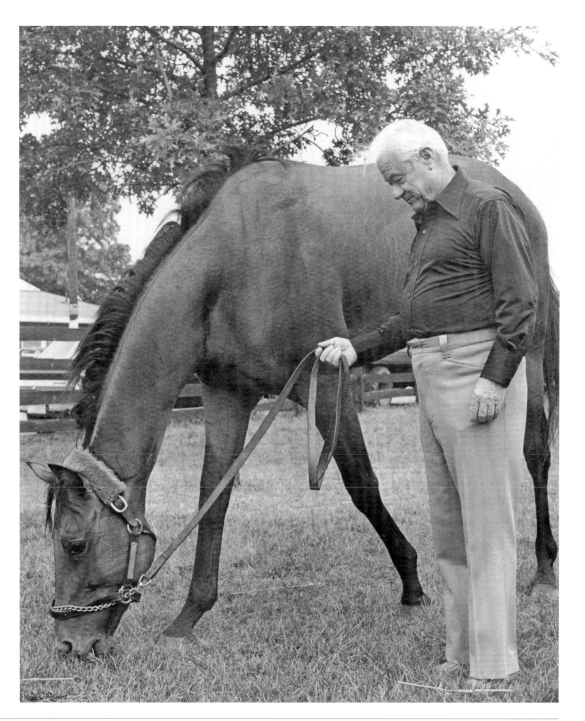

OPPOSITE LEFT: Amory L. Haskell (left) presents the 1956 Monmouth Handicap trophy to the winning connections of Nashua. Nashua was trained by "Sunny Jim" Fitzsimmons, ridden by Eddie Arcaro (center) and owned by Leslie Combs II. Combs acquired Nashua prior to his four-year-old season for slightly more than $1,250,000 at the 1955 dispersal of the Woodward Thoroughbred holdings.

OPPOSITE RIGHT: Nashua grazes at Monmouth Park. His archrival, Swaps, stole Nashua's opportunity for the 1955 Triple Crown when he won the Kentucky Derby. Nashua finished second in the Derby, but went on to win the Preakness and Belmont Stakes. Nashua earned Horse of the Year honors and was Champion Three-Year-Old that year.

ABOVE: Sword Dancer in a morning workout at Monmouth Park. Sword Dancer won the 1959 Monmouth Handicap with Hall of Fame jockey Willie Shoemaker in the irons. He won Horse of the Year honors after capping that season with a seven-length win against older horses in the two-mile Jockey Club Gold Cup.

RIGHT: Riva Ridge grazes at Monmouth Park with his Hall of Fame trainer Lucien Laurin. He finished a disappointing 4th in the 1972 Monmouth Handicap as the favorite. Riva Ridge started as the favorite in 22 of his 30 lifetime starts. He amassed 17 victories including the 1972 Kentucky Derby and Belmont Stakes.

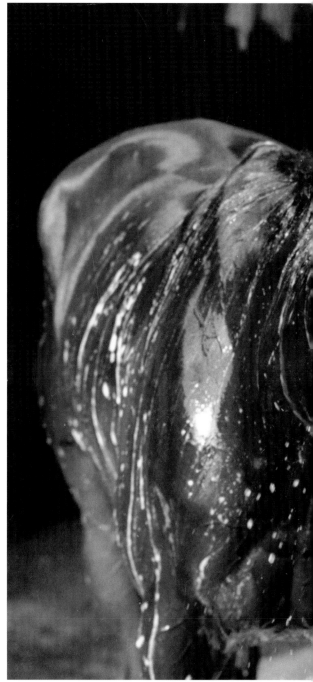

OPPOSITE: Skip Away returns to the winner's circle with Jerry Bailey after winning the 1998 Philip H. Iselin Handicap as a five-year-old. His first attempt at the Iselin was unsuccessful when he finished 2nd to Formal Gold the year prior. Skip Away won the 1996 Haskell Invitational under Jose Santos. His sire, Skip Trial won the Haskell in 1985.

LEFT: Silverbulletday receives a morning bath. She earned Champion Filly honors as a two-year-old (1998) and again as a three-year-old (1999).

ABOVE: Silverbulletday cruises to a five-length victory in the Monmouth Oaks under jockey Jerry Bailey. Trained by Bob Baffert and owned by Mike Pegram, Silverbulletday won 14 of 18 starts.

FOLLOWING LEFT: Trainer Jimmy Croll, Jr. with his champion Holy Bull in 1994. Croll acquired Holy Bull when a longtime client, Rachel Carpenter, left the colt to him in her will.

FOLLOWING MIDDLE: Holy Bull and Mike Smith romp in the 1994 Haskell Invitational. He only suffered three losses (including the Kentucky Derby) in his 16-race career. The grey horse would go on to capture 1994 Horse of the Year honors. Holy Bull's victory in the Haskell Invitational marked the third time his trainer, Jimmy Croll, Jr. won the race. His first Haskell victory came 25 years prior with Al Hattab and his second came in 1987 with Bet Twice.

FOLLOWING TOP RIGHT: Open Mind returns to the winner's circle after winning the 1988 New Jersey Breeders' Stakes in only her second career start. Open Mind was bred in New Jersey by Due Process Stables and broke her maiden at Monmouth Park. Among her many accomplishments were victories in the Breeders' Cup Juvenile Fillies, the Kentucky Oaks and the Triple Tiara (the Mother Goose Stakes, the Coaching Club American Oaks and the Alabama Stakes).

FOLLOWING BOTTOM RIGHT: Personal Ensign, with Randy Romero riding, wins the 1988 Molly Pitcher Handicap.

Monmouth Park

HASKELL INVITATIONAL

The Haskell. No other race in Monmouth Park history showcases the Sport of Kings as well as the Grade I, $1,000,000 Haskell Invitational, the richest invitational in North America. The cornerstone of the Monmouth Park season, the Haskell is an "invitation only" event - at least for the horses. The elite three-year-olds in the country are extended invitations to compete in this mile-and-an-eighth race.

The champions have not disappointed. In its relatively short history of just over 40 years, the Haskell has played host to 20 champions, among them six Horse of the Year winners. Spend a Buck, Alysheba, Holy Bull, Skip Away, Point Given and Curlin all included the Haskell on their racing calendars. However, not all were successful. Spend a Buck was beaten by Skip Trial (sire of Skip Away), and Alysheba finished second to his archrival Bet Twice. Curlin finished third in the 2007 edition of the Haskell, but then returned to Monmouth for ultimate redemption with a victory in the 2007 Breeders' Cup Classic. Regardless of how the champions fare, there is always the promise of an exciting performance, the promise of a great race.

The Haskell has not only become a can't miss event for the horses but also for racing fans. Ticket requests come in even before the season opens, and on the first Sunday in August more than 40,000 fans pack the stands to see history in the making.

If you take a summer stroll down the local boardwalk, you are sure to catch sight of the signature Haskell Hat. The Haskell Hat giveaway began in 1988 and those who have collected each year's hat are held in high regard by their racing friends. Fans proudly sport the symbol of Monmouth Park's most prestigious race - the Haskell… *where champions prove their greatness.* ■

LEFT: Jockey Pat Day gallantly struggles under the weight of the Haskell Trophy after winning in 1999 on Menifee.

RIGHT: Bet Twice, with Craig Perret up, wins the 1987 Haskell over Alysheba and Lost Code. *Reprinted with permission, Courtesy, Asbury Park Press, a Gannett Co. newspaper*

ABOVE: The Haskell Invitational Trophy.

RIGHT: Haskell logos from 2006-2008.

THIS PAGE: The traditional Haskell Hat from 1988 to 2007.

TOP: Forty Niner, Champion Two-Year-Old Colt of 1987, captures the 1988 Haskell. Laffit Pincay, Jr. piloted the chestnut to a nose victory over Seeking the Gold and jockey Pat Day.

RIGHT: King Glorious powers home under Chris McCarron to win the 1989 Haskell.

ABOVE: Restless Con, with Tim Doocy aboard, wins the 1990 Haskell over Baron de Vaux.

LEFT: Lost Mountain (left), with Craig Perret aboard, triumphs over Corporate Report and Hall of Champions member Hansel in the 1991 Haskell. Craig Perret rode in the Haskell an unmatched 13 times, winning three times (1981, 1987, and 1991).

BELOW: Technology easily wins the 1992 Haskell under jockey Jerry Bailey, who has won two Haskells (1992, 2005) from seven mounts.

BELOW LEFT: Kissin Kris cruises under the wire with Jose Santos aboard in the 1993 Haskell.

BOTTOM: Mike Smith and Holy Bull after winning the 1994 Haskell. Holy Bull won Horse of the Year honors as well as Champion Three-Year-Old the same year.

RIGHT: Serena's Song becomes the first filly to win the Haskell. Hall of Fame jockey Gary Stevens piloted the filly for her triumph over the colts in the 1995 renewal.

BELOW: Skip Away carries Jose Santos to his second Haskell victory in the 1996 edition of the race. Skip Away's sire, Skip Trial won the Haskell in 1985.

ABOVE LEFT: Touch Gold, with Chris McCarron aboard, puts away Anet and Free House in the 1997 Haskell.

LEFT: Touch Gold takes flight down the homestretch.

ABOVE: Touch Gold returns to the winner's circle with Chris McCarron. McCarron retired with 7,141 winners and in 1989 was inducted into the Hall of Fame.

TOP: Coronado's Quest, with Mike Smith riding, wins the 1998 Haskell over Belmont Stakes winner Victory Gallop. His sire, Forty Niner, won the 1988 Haskell.

ABOVE: Menifee, with Pat Day aboard, scores over Cat Thief in the 1999 Haskell.

RIGHT: Jockey Alex Solis celebrates his 2000 Haskell victory aboard Dixie Union.

LEFT: Point Given (left with blinkers) and Gary Stevens drive past Touch Tone (right) and Burning Roma (center) to win the 2001 Haskell. Stevens also won the 1995 edition of the Haskell with the filly Serena's Song.

ABOVE: Point Given keeps a watchful eye on things from his stall at Monmouth Park. Point Given won four consecutive $1 million races: the Preakness Stakes, Belmont Stakes, Haskell and Travers Stakes, all en route to Horse of the Year honors.

ABOVE: War Emblem, the first Kentucky Derby-Haskell winner in Monmouth history, comes under the wire with jockey Victor Espinoza in the 2002 Haskell.

RIGHT: War Emblem defeats Magic Weisner and Like a Hero in the 2002 Haskell. War Emblem won the Kentucky Derby and Preakness, but was denied the Triple Crown after stumbling badly at the start of the Belmont Stakes.

ABOVE RIGHT: Peace Rules, under Edgar Prado, leads the field out of the final turn en route to victory in the 2003 Haskell. Peace Rules defeated three-year-old Champion Funny Cide (3rd) in front of a record Haskell crowd of 53,638.

ABOVE & RIGHT: Lion Heart gives Joe Bravo his first Haskell win in 2004.

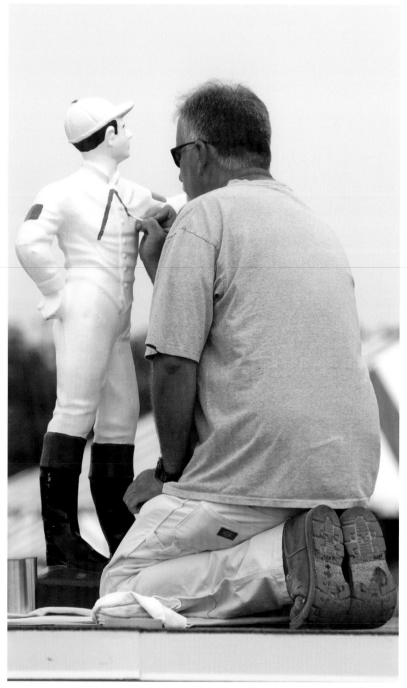

ABOVE: Co-owners Dave Shimmon (left) and Bill Bianco (right) guide Roman Ruler and Jerry Bailey into the winner's circle after winning the 2005 Haskell.

RIGHT: The winning owner's colors are painted on the Haskell jockey. The Haskell jockey statues can be found throughout the park.

OPPOSITE: Bluegrass Cat (center), under John Velazquez, heads competitor Praying For Cash (right) before drawing away to a seven-length victory in the 2006 Haskell – the largest winning margin in the history of the race.

LEFT & ABOVE: Any Given Saturday, with Garret Gomez up, gives fans a feeling of déjà vu in the 2007 Haskell. The win marked back-to-back victories for the winning connections, trainer Todd Pletcher and owner WinStar Farm. Hard Spun finished second and the eventual Horse of the Year, Curlin, was third. Curlin returned to Monmouth Park to triumph in the 2007 Breeders' Cup Classic.

BREEDERS' CUP

The Breeders' Cup World Championships is the single greatest event in Thoroughbred racing. It is the culmination of the racing season when the best horses of each division are brought together to compete and to determine who is to be crowned Champion.

Inaugurated in 1984, the Breeders' Cup World Championships have been hosted by ten different tracks in the United States and Canada. In 2007, Monmouth Park became the most recent track to have the honor of hosting the Breeders' Cup, joining Aqueduct, Arlington Park, Belmont Park, Churchill Downs, Gulfstream Park, Hollywood Park, Lone Star Park, Santa Anita Park and Woodbine.

Monmouth Park won the bid to host the Breeders' Cup nearly three years prior to the event. In those three years, the aging facility received a well-deserved facelift and underwent $30 million in renovations including a new turf course, resurfaced dirt track, state-of-the-art teletheater and countless other improvements.

The 2007 Breeders' Cup World Championships, the first ever two-day event in Breeders' Cup history, was the pinnacle of achievement for the shore's greatest stretch. With its rich history of champions, it was only fitting that the best horses in the world be brought to Monmouth Park to stake their claim as one of racing's immortals.

The 60,000 fans that braved the fateful weather those two days in late October were treated to the best that racing had to offer. Curlin defeated his foes and clinched Horse of the Year honors with a dominating victory in the Breeders' Cup Classic, while the darling of the Monmouth Park turf, English Channel, secured Champion Turf Horse honors with a victory in the Breeders' Cup Turf. In total, eight winners – War Pass, Indian Blessing, Lahudood, Midnight Lute, Ginger Punch, Maryfield, English Channel and Curlin secured Champion honors based on their Breeders' Cup performances. ■

LEFT: Curlin (left) takes on Hard Spun (center) and Street Sense (right) in the 2007 Breeders' Cup Classic. Robby Albarado guided the big chestnut to a dominating victory in the $5,000,000 race.

OPPOSITE: A beautiful morning at Monmouth Park during the week leading up to the Breeders' Cup. The green temporary stadium seats stretch the length of the homestretch. Nearly 20,000 temporary seats were installed for the event.

LEFT: Jockey Calvin Borel high-fives regular exercise rider Tracey Wilkes after Street Sense worked the Tuesday prior to the Breeders' Cup Classic. Guiding Street Sense off the track is Paul Rutherford.

ABOVE: Long hair falls over the eye of a Thoroughbred.

BELOW: The Official Track Programs from the two-day Breeders' Cup. The Breeders' Cup was expanded to a two-day event for the first time in 2007.

ABOVE: Breeders' Cup tickets for Saturday, October 27, 2007.

RIGHT: The Breeders' Cup statue adorns the paddock.

OPPOSITE LEFT: Images of racing's richest day.

OPPOSITE TOP RIGHT: The Breeders' Cup Classic garland of flowers.

OPPOSITE BOTTOM RIGHT: The 2007 Breeders' Cup World Championships logo designed to capture the Jersey Shore and Monmouth Park.

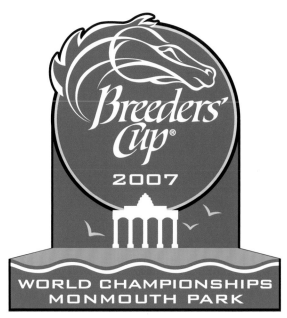

OPPOSITE TOP LEFT: Staying dry under an umbrella hat.

OPPOSITE MIDDLE LEFT: A couple enjoying the Breeders' Cup at Monmouth Park.

OPPOSITE BOTTOM LEFT: A fan watches the action.

OPPOSITE RIGHT: Chuck C. Lopez signs an autograph for a happy patron.

ABOVE: Fans consult the *Daily Racing Form*.

RIGHT: Jockey Rajiv Maragh makes his way through the mud after a race.

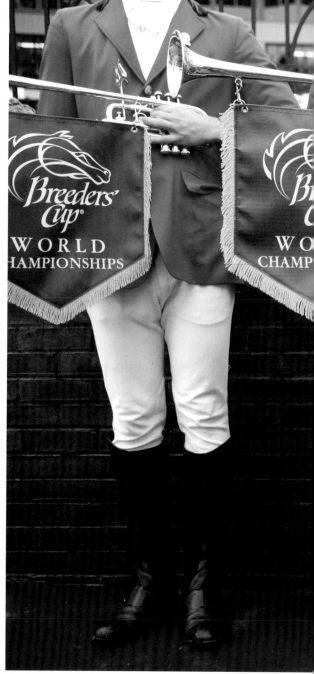

ABOVE: Bugler Mark O'Keefe calls the horses to the post.

RIGHT: The All Star Buglers stand ready to perform.

OPPOSITE: The outrider's pony keeps an eye on things.

FOLLOWING LEFT: Racing fans by the paddock enjoy a brief moment of sun.

FOLLOWING RIGHT: The Breeders' Cup Distaff field thunders through the slop.

OPPOSITE TOP LEFT & BOTTOM LEFT: Maryfield, with Elvis Trujillo up, wins the inaugural running of the $1,000,000 Breeders' Cup Filly and Mare Sprint.

OPPOSITE TOP RIGHT: Julien Leparoux celebrates his victory aboard Nownownow in the $1,000,000 Breeders' Cup Juvenile Turf.

OPPOSITE BOTTOM RIGHT: Julien Leparoux and Nownownow overcome Achill Island (inside) to win the inaugural running of the $1,000,000 Breeders' Cup Juvenile Turf.

LEFT: Corinthian in the winner's circle after winning the inaugural running of the $1,000,000 Breeders' Cup Dirt Mile.

ABOVE: Corinthian, with Kent Desormeaux in the irons, skips through the slop to win the $1,000,000 Breeders' Cup Dirt Mile for trainer James A. "Jimmy" Jerkens and owner Centennial Farms.

ABOVE: An exuberant fan flashes his sign for the camera.

LEFT: A representative from Emirates Airlines, sponsor of the $2,000,000 Breeders' Cup Filly & Mare Turf and the $2,000,000 Breeders' Cup Distaff.

OPPOSITE LEFT: Indian Blessing (far right) leads the field to the first turn in the $2,000,000 Breeders' Cup Juvenile Fillies. Trained by Bob Baffert, Indian Blessing went wire-to-wire to win the Juvenile Fillies for owners Patti and Hal J. Earnhardt, III.

OPPOSITE RIGHT: Garrett Gomez celebrates his victory aboard Indian Blessing, who capped her undefeated season with an Eclipse Award as Champion Two-Year-Old Filly.

ABOVE: War Pass wins the $2,000,000 Breeders' Cup Juvenile geared down under jockey Cornelio Velasquez. War Pass was trained by Nick Zito for owner Robert LaPenta.

RIGHT: War Pass leads the field into the first turn with Globalization (left) and Z Humor (right) hot on his heels. War Pass was voted Champion Two-Year-Old Colt after an undefeated season.

OPPOSITE TOP LEFT: Alan Garcia drives home Lahudood in the $2,000,000 Breeders' Cup Filly & Mare Turf to register a victory over Honey Ryder (left).

OPPOSITE BOTTOM LEFT: Lahudood (blue and white silks) relishes the soft going in the Breeders' Cup Filly & Mare Turf.

OPPOSITE RIGHT: Jockey Alan Garcia smiles happily after his Breeders' Cup win for trainer Kiaran McLaughlin and owner Shadwell Farm.

OPPOSITE: Garrett Gomez raises his whip after his Breeders' Cup victory aboard Midnight Lute in the $2,000,000 Breeders' Cup Sprint.

ABOVE: A young fan enjoys the races from the perfect vantage point.

RIGHT: Garret Gomez gives the thumbs-up after winning the Breeders' Cup Sprint. Midnight Lute was trained by Bob Baffert and owned by Mike Pegram and Watson & Weitman Performance.

Monmouth Park

OPPOSITE: Kip Deville carries the colors of IEAH Stables, A. Cohen, J. Roberts, S. Cohen, R. Cobb & D. Robertson under the wire.

FAR LEFT: Kip Deville, with Cornelio Velasquez in the irons, wins the $2,000,000 Breeders' Cup Mile.

ABOVE: Kip Deville carries his garland of purple and gold flowers into the winner's circle.

LEFT: Trainer Rick Dutrow, Jr. celebrates his victory.

LEFT: Ginger Punch, with Rafael Bejarano up, wins the $2,000,000 Breeders' Cup Distaff over Hystericalady.

ABOVE: Rafael Bejarano celebrates his victory. Ginger Punch was trained by Robert "Bobby" Frankel for Stronach Stables.

OPPOSITE LEFT: Frank Stronach, owner of Ginger Punch, raises his Breeders' Cup trophy. Ginger Punch went on to win the Eclipse Award as Champion Older Female.

OPPOSITE RIGHT: Racing fans watch the races from the Parterre boxes. The traditional white and red geraniums were replaced with purple and gold mums for the Breeders' Cup.

OPPOSITE: A two-time winner of the Grade I United Nations, English Channel, under John Velazquez, romps to a dominating victory in the $3,000,000 Breeders' Cup Turf.

FAR LEFT TOP: English Channel wins the $3,000,000 Breeders' Cup Turf.

FAR LEFT MIDDLE: A family cheers the runners home.

FAR LEFT BOTTOM: A young fan points out his favorite.

LEFT: Owner Jim Scatuorchio checks out the mud as he waits for English Channel to return to the winner's circle after winning the Breeders' Cup Turf. Scatuorchio is a long-time supporter of Monmouth Park and a New Jersey native.

BELOW: English Channel sports the garland of flowers for his victory in the Breeders' Cup Turf. English Channel topped his fantastic season with an Eclipse Award as Champion Turf Horse.

OPPOSITE: The field breaks from the starting gate in the $5,000,000 Breeders' Cup Classic.

LEFT: Robby Albarado waves his whip in victory aboard Curlin after winning the Breeders' Cup Classic.

ABOVE: Curlin shines in the reflection of the photo finish mirror. Curlin was 4-1/2 lengths clear of Hard Spun. Awesome Gem rallied for third and Kentucky Derby winner Street Sense finished fourth.

OPPOSITE: Curlin was trained by Steve Asmussen for owners Midnight Cry, Padua Stables, Stonestreet Stables & George Bolton.

LEFT: Curlin is escorted into the winner's circle following his Breeders' Cup Classic victory.

ABOVE: Scott Blasi, assistant trainer to Steve Asmussen, celebrates Curlin's Classic win.

FOLLOWING: Monmouth Park glows brightly in the aftermath of the Breeders' Cup World Championships.
Courtesy Bo Baumgartner Photography